21.56

CONNECTICUT

The Constitution State

Derek Miller, Michael Burgan,
Stephanie Fitzgerald, and Gerry Boehme

Cavendish
Square

New York

Published in 2020 by Cavendish Square Publishing, LLC
243 5th Avenue, Suite 136, New York, NY 10016

Library of Congress Cataloging-in-Publication Data

Names: Miller, Derek, author. | Burgan, Michael, author. | Fitzgerald, Stephanie, author. | Boehme, Gerry, author.
Title: Connecticut / Derek Miller, Michael Burgan, Stephanie Fitzgerald, and Gerry Boehme.
Description: Fourth edition. | New York : Cavendish Square, 2020. |
Series: It's my state! | Includes bibliographical references and index.
Identifiers: LCCN 2018045929 (print) | LCCN 2018046527 (ebook) |
ISBN 9781502641779 (ebook) | ISBN 9781502641762 (library bound) | ISBN 9781502644527 (pbk.)
Subjects: LCSH: Connecticut--Juvenile literature.
Classification: LCC F94.3 (ebook) | LCC F94.3 .B87 2020 (print) | DDC 974.6--dc23
LC record available at https://lccn.loc.gov/2018045929

Editorial Director: David McNamara
Editor: Caitlyn Miller
Copy Editor: Nathan Heidelberger
Associate Art Director: Alan Sliwinski
Designer: Jessica Nevins
Production Coordinator: Karol Szymczuk
Photo Research: J8 Media

Printed in the United States of America

It's My
STATE!

Table of Contents

SNAPSHOT
CONNECTICUT

The Constitution State

Statehood

January 9, 1788

Population

3,588,184
(2017 census estimate)

Capital

Hartford

State Seal

The Great Seal of the State of Connecticut dates to the year 1784. Three grapevines stand in the center of an oval. On a blue ribbon under the grapevines is the state motto, "Qui Transtulit Sustinet," which means "He who transplanted still sustains." The motto dates to colonial times, when Connecticut was full of transplants from Great Britain.

State Flag

Connecticut's flag shares some elements with its seal. It features the same motto as the seal and the same three grape vines. However, they appear on a white shield rather than inside an oval. This shield display is known as the state's "armorial bearings." The background color of the flag is azure blue.

State Song

"Yankee Doodle" was adopted as Connecticut's state song in 1978. The popular American song dates to the era of the Revolutionary War. It was first used by the British to mock the American colonists. Americans soon adopted the song as their own. When the British army surrendered at the Battle of Saratoga in 1777, American soldiers played "Yankee Doodle."

HISTORICAL EVENTS TIMELINE

1614

Adriaen Block is the first European to sail up the Connecticut River. Trade soon begins between the Dutch and Native Americans in the area.

1636

Thomas Hooker leads a group of Puritans from Massachusetts to establish a new settlement at Hartford.

1637

English colonists defeat local Native Americans and end of the Pequot War.

State Tree

The Charter Oak is the state tree. It played an important part in early Connecticut history. In 1662, Connecticut was given a royal charter by King Charles II. His brother, James II, later regretted this. In 1687, he sent a representative to take back the charter. According to legend, the document was hidden in the Charter Oak to protect it. The Charter Oak later fell in 1856, but it remains the state tree to this day.

State Flower

The mountain laurel was designated as Connecticut's state flower in 1907. The shrub can be found across the state. Its white and pink blossoms bloom in early summer. The flowers are well known for their beauty, and mountain laurels are a common ornamental plant in the United States and Europe.

1639

The Fundamental Orders, North America's first written constitution, is signed in Connecticut.

1788

Connecticut approves the US Constitution and becomes the fifth state to join the new nation.

1794

Connecticut native Eli Whitney receives a patent for the cotton gin. It quickly separates cotton seeds from fibers, increasing the economic importance of cotton.

State Insect

European Mantis

1954

The world's first nuclear-powered submarine is launched from Groton, Connecticut. Later, after its service in the US Navy, it returns to Groton as a museum ship.

1975

Ella Grasso is sworn in as the first female governor of Connecticut. She is the fourth female governor in United States history.

2001

Hartford breaks ground on Adriaen's Landing, a project designed to develop the downtown area.

State Aircraft
F4U Corsair

State Shellfish
Eastern Oyster

CURRENT EVENTS TIMELINE

2004

The men's and women's teams of the University of Connecticut both win the NCAA Division I Basketball Championships in the same season, making history.

2012

Hurricane Sandy impacts Connecticut, leading to five deaths in the state and massive amounts of property damage.

2017

A blizzard in March dumps more than 2 feet (61 centimeters) of snow on some areas of Connecticut and leaves many people without power.

The Housatonic
River flows through
western Connecticut.

Geography

Rolling hills, farmland, forests, and scenic rivers blanket Connecticut. Spectacular waterfalls and beautiful autumn **foliage** draw visitors to the state's natural beauty. At its southern edge, Connecticut meets Long Island Sound with sandy beaches and rocky coastlines. This important waterway gives the state access to the ocean and played an important role in both the state's history and its modern economy. The beautiful scenery of the state has something for everyone.

The Regions of Connecticut

The surface of Connecticut was formed over millions of years. About eighteen thousand years ago, large masses of ice called glaciers covered what is now Connecticut as well as other parts of North America. As the glaciers moved, they carved out valleys. When the ice began to melt, soil and rocks were deposited across the land, helping to shape hills and other rocky features.

Today, Connecticut can be divided into four major regions: the Central Valley, the Coastal Lowlands, the Western Uplands, and

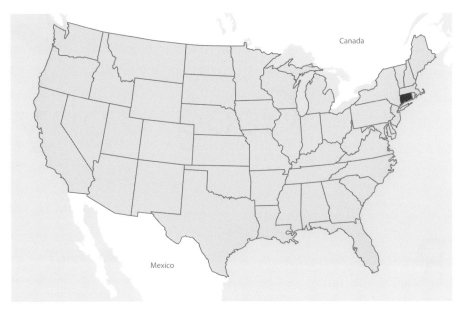

Canada

Mexico

Connecticut borders Massachusetts, Rhode Island, and New York.

the Eastern Uplands. In general, the eastern and western portions of Connecticut are very rocky and not suited for farming, while the central portion of the state contains a fertile valley.

The Central Valley

The Connecticut River dominates the center of the state. At 410 miles (660 kilometers) long, it is the longest river in New England. The river starts in a small beaver pond near the border between New Hampshire and Canada. Moving south, it divides New Hampshire and Vermont. It then passes through Massachusetts and Connecticut. The Connecticut River's course is fairly straight in the northern half of the state before it twists and turns down to Long Island Sound. Shallow waters and sandbars—ridges of sand formed by waves and currents—make it hard to sail at the mouth of the river. Unlike many large American rivers, the Connecticut River does not have a major port or city at its mouth. Still, the river has been an important waterway for moving goods and people.

The land on either side of the river is called the Connecticut Valley, or Central Valley. Water from the river makes the valley perfect for growing crops. Native peoples from various tribes were the first to farm this land. The rich farmland later drew Europeans to the area. Connecticut's capital, Hartford, sits on the western bank of the river.

Hartford is home to nearly 125,000 people.

The Coastal Lowlands

The Connecticut River travels south until it empties into Long Island Sound. The land that stretches along the length of the sound forms another region of Connecticut called the Coastal Lowlands, or Coastal Slope. The land here is mostly flat, with marshlands and small coves that cut into the shoreline.

By the 1960s, pollution choked the waters of the Connecticut River and affected Long Island Sound as well. Factories and towns had been dumping waste into the river for more than one hundred years, killing animals and plants that live in the water. The New England states and the US government have spent millions of dollars to clean up the river. Today, some sections are clean enough for swimming and fishing.

The Western Uplands

Hills dot the landscape in the area west of the river called the Western Uplands. The northwest corner of the state includes Connecticut's highest point, the southern side of Mount Frissell, which

FAST FACT

Connecticut is the third-smallest state in the country. It is roughly rectangular and measures 110 miles (177 km) across and 70 miles (112 km) top to bottom at its broadest. Only the states of Rhode Island and Delaware are smaller.

Connecticut's Biggest Cities

(Population numbers are from the US Census Bureau's 2017 projections for incorporated cities.)

Bridgeport

New Haven

1. Bridgeport: population 146,579

Bridgeport sits on Long Island Sound and is home to thirteen officially delineated neighborhoods. Attractions include shoreline parks, museums, regional baseball and hockey, festivals, and national musical performances.

2. New Haven: population 131,014

Also located on the northern shore of Long Island Sound, New Haven is the home of Yale University. The city served as co-capital of Connecticut from 1701 until 1873, when Hartford was chosen as the centralized state capital.

3. Stamford: population 130,824

In recent years, Stamford has grown impressively. Stamford businesses include leaders in finance, pharmaceuticals, insurance, hospitality, media, and consumer products. The Stamford Transportation Center includes the busiest train station between New York City and Boston.

4. Hartford: population 123,400

Hartford is Connecticut's capital and is the birthplace of the Boys and Girls Clubs of America. Hartford has been nicknamed the "Insurance Capital of the World" because a number of important insurance companies got their start in the city. Hartford was founded in 1636 and ranks among the oldest cities in the United States.

5. Waterbury: population 108,629

Once the leading center in the United States for the manufacture of brassware, Waterbury was nicknamed "The Brass City." In 1932, the Waterbury Clock Company, now known as Timex, partnered with Disney on Mickey Mouse watches and clocks. Its huge success saved the company from bankruptcy.

6. Norwalk: population 89,005

Norwalk is located along the Connecticut coast between Bridgeport and Stamford. Known for its oysters, Norwalk hosts an annual Oyster Festival just after Labor Day.

Norwalk

7. Danbury: population 85,246

Danbury is in Fairfield County in southwest Connecticut and is close to Candlewood Lake, the largest lake in the state. Its location allows easy access to big-city activities as well as small-town New England traditions.

8. New Britain: population 72,710

Only 9 miles (14 km) away from Hartford, New Britain is known for manufacturing hardware and tools. The city has the largest Polish population in the state and features the oldest museum in the United States for American art.

9. Bristol: population 60,223

Located 20 miles (32 km) southwest of Hartford, Bristol is well known as the home of ESPN and Lake Compounce, America's oldest operating theme park.

10. Meriden: population 59,927

Calling itself the "Crossroads of Connecticut," Meriden is just two hours from Boston and New York City. It is also midway between New Haven and Hartford. Every April, the Meriden Daffodil Festival draws visitors with its crafts and entertainment, including a fireworks show and carnival rides.

reaches a height of 2,380 feet (725 meters). Mount Frissell is part of a region called the Berkshire Hills. Most of this mountain, including its peak, is located in Massachusetts.

Bear Mountain is the tallest peak located entirely within Connecticut's borders, standing 2,323 feet (708 m) high. It is located just east of Mount Frissell. The Appalachian Trail, which stretches from Georgia to Maine, crosses Bear Mountain.

The Western Uplands contain one major river, the Housatonic. It begins in Massachusetts and runs through the western section of Connecticut before draining into Long Island Sound. The Housatonic's fast-moving waters once provided power for many mills and factories by running generators that created electricity. This kind of electricity is called hydroelectricity, or hydropower.

The state's two largest lakes are also in this region. Candlewood Lake and Barkhamsted Reservoir were not made by natural forces, but by

Candlewood Lake is the largest lake in Connecticut.

people. Candlewood Lake, Connecticut's largest lake, was created in 1928 to provide hydroelectric power. The lake is also very popular with Connecticut residents and visitors. The lake has 60 miles (97 km) of shoreline and cuts through several towns. Many people have homes along its peaceful shores, with boaters and swimmers filling the lake in the warmer months.

The western town of Kent is home to Kent Falls, a state park that features the highest waterfall in Connecticut. It drops around 250 feet (76 m). Visitors hike and picnic along trails in the park.

Kent Falls

The Eastern Uplands

The region east of the Connecticut River is called the Eastern Uplands. The Eastern Uplands are not quite as high as the Western Uplands. Some spots have many hills, but in other places, flat areas of land are used for farming and raising dairy cows. The US government maintains a major naval submarine base at the mouth of the Thames River in New London.

"To the South Sea"

Today, Connecticut is the third-smallest state. But at one point, the small state claimed a vast amount of territory, stretching all the way across North America to the Pacific Ocean! This claim rested on the Charter of 1662—the document that was hidden in the Charter Oak and gave the famous tree its name. The charter defined the colony of Connecticut as stretching "From the said Narraganset-Bay on the East, to the South Sea on the West Part." The South Sea is now known as the Pacific Ocean. King Charles II, who granted the charter, did not know that the distance between the Narraganset Bay and the Pacific was more than 2,500 miles (4000 km). From north to south, Connecticut was just 70 miles (112 km)!

Charles II later granted William Penn a portion of this same land that was given to Connecticut in its charter. A large stretch of land was now claimed by Pennsylvania and Connecticut. Settlers loyal to Penn (called Pennamites) and settlers from Connecticut soon set up opposing towns and forts. The situation was tense, with landowners on either side sometimes claiming the same land. Violence eventually broke out, and between 1769 and 1784 three Pennamite-Yankee wars were fought. There were relatively few deaths, but militias burned farms and forced out settlers. The situation was finally resolved in 1799. The territory was given to Pennsylvania, but the Yankee settlers were allowed to keep their land and farms.

Later Border Disputes

Western claims were not the only border disputes in Connecticut history. There were also conflicts with Massachusetts and New York. The border between Connecticut and Massachusetts was first surveyed in 1642. However, the two men who surveyed it were sailors and were not qualified for the task. They did not even walk the border they were supposed to decide. Instead, they sailed around it and up a nearby river. The resulting survey was nowhere near the correct place, and Connecticut towns were placed in Massachusetts. When the line was resurveyed decades later, Massachusetts refused to acknowledge it at first. The situation was eventually resolved peacefully, and by 1826 the modern-day boundary was largely agreed on.

The border dispute with New York was settled through a compromise. Connecticut desired the land on which Greenwich was built. Settlers there considered themselves Nutmeggers (the nickname for Connecticut's residents). In return, they gave New York a comparable sliver of land, known as the "Oblong," stretching along their shared border. This peaceful settlement was signed by both states in 1683. This is how Connecticut got its distinctive southwestern panhandle.

King Charles II granted the Charter of 1662, which created the colony of Connecticut.

Connecticut is known for its eye-catching fall leaves.

Climate

The weather in Connecticut changes with the seasons. In summer, the air can be humid, and temperatures can rise above 90 degrees Fahrenheit (32 degrees Celsius). Autumn tends to be cool and sunny, as the leaves change from green to red, yellow, and gold. In the winter, parts of the state can get more than 4 feet (1.2 m) of snow, but temperatures are usually not bitterly cold. In general, the western hills receive more snow and have colder weather than the rest of the state.

Strong winds and waves from storms can strike at any time of the year, damaging houses and flooding roads along Long Island Sound. Connecticut is sometimes hit by nor'easters, large storms that form when northern and southern storm fronts collide. The amount of snow or rain from one nor'easter can vary quite a bit from north to south. The Western Uplands might receive as much as 1 foot (30 cm) of snow, while the shoreline is hit only with rain. Flooding can also occur early in the spring, when melting snow along the Connecticut River raises the water level and floods nearby land.

Visiting Mystic

The small village of Mystic draws many tourists to Connecticut. The area has a long **maritime** history. Its harbor made it a safe port for ships in early American history, and a large shipbuilding industry grew there. In 1929, the Mystic Seaport Museum was founded to celebrate this rich tradition. The museum grew into one of the most important maritime museums in the country. Today, visitors can see hundreds of historic ships there, including the 1841 whaleship *Charles W. Morgan.* Photographs, videos, and artifacts also document the area's maritime history.

Open since 1929, Mystic Seaport Museum brings visitors from all over.

Mystic is also home to the Mystic Aquarium—another one of Connecticut's important tourist sites. The Mystic Aquarium is the only New England aquarium that houses beluga whales. Visitors can see them and a wide range of other aquatic animals. The mission of the Mystic Aquarium is to inspire visitors to care more about protecting and learning about life in our planet's oceans.

In addition to the Mystic Seaport Museum and Mystic Aquarium, the town of Mystic itself is a draw for tourists. It is a picturesque New England village, full of local shops and restaurants. It makes the perfect vacation spot for visitors looking to escape the nearby big cities of Boston and New York.

Tourists interact with beluga whales at Mystic Aquarium.

Male white-tailed deer shed their antlers each year.

Wildlife

Forests cover around 60 percent of Connecticut, and the state is home to many kinds of trees, flowers, and other plants. Oak, maple, and ash are some of the common leafy trees that grow in the state. Evergreen trees, such as pine and fir, also are common.

Many different kinds of animals live in these forests and nearby fields. One of the most common mammals is the white-tailed deer. Farmers and homeowners use wire fences or special plantings to help stop deer from eating crops as well as other plants and shrubs. Connecticut also allows deer hunting in certain seasons to prevent some animals from overpopulating.

Some animals that once lived in Connecticut left the region or died off as people cut down forests to build homes. In recent years, some of these animals, such as coyotes, have returned to the state. Families are now warned to keep their pets in at night, so they will not become dinner for any prowling coyotes.

Common birds in Connecticut include robins, sparrows, and crows. The number of wild turkeys roaming through the forests— or across backyards—continues to rise. Bald eagles also live in the state, though they are few and are considered threatened.

Many different types of fish swim in Connecticut's waters. Among them is the shad. The roe, or eggs, of this fish are considered a dinner treat. Each May, the town of Windsor has a festival honoring the shad.

Along Long Island Sound, fishers catch shellfish such as lobsters and oysters. Oysters from Connecticut are very popular. In 1997 and 1998, however, a sudden rise in the water temperature almost destroyed Connecticut's oyster fishing industry. The higher temperature encouraged the growth of small deadly organisms that target oysters. Thousands of acres of shellfish were killed. To prevent this kind of disaster from happening again, marine biologists are breeding hardier, parasite-resistant oysters. In the twenty-first century, Connecticut's oyster industry is enjoying a slow but steady recovery.

Endangered Animals

Some animals in Connecticut are considered endangered. This means that their numbers are very small and that they are at risk of disappearing completely. When an animal or plant is listed as endangered, it becomes illegal to kill it or hurt its habitat.

The peregrine falcon is an example of an endangered bird in the state. One of the world's fastest birds, they can reach speeds of 175 miles per hour (282 kilometers per hour)

Peregrine falcons hunt birds and bats.

when diving for food. Peregrines were once common in Connecticut and the rest of North America. However, by 1950 none of these birds were left in the state. They suffered from the use of chemical pesticides and later joined the national list of endangered animals.

The US government worked to increase the number of peregrines. It raised babies and then released them in the wild. In 1997, a pair of peregrine falcons settled in Hartford. They built a nest on the Travelers Tower, one of the state's tallest buildings. The pair then had chicks. The following year, more peregrines returned to Hartford, and several others built nests in nearby cities. Although the peregrine falcon is no longer on the national list of endangered animals, the state of Connecticut still considers it threatened.

While some animals are threatened in Connecticut, others are coming to the state for the first time. In the 1990s, moose began to take up residence in the state. They were spreading southward into the region. It is unclear if moose used to live in the state during colonial times. They may have been driven out by early settlers. Alternatively, they may have never called the state home until recent years. Today, there are an estimated one hundred moose in Connecticut.

Moose have started making a home in Connecticut in recent years.

What Lives in Connecticut?

Flora

Black Birch This medium-sized tree is found across Connecticut. In the autumn, its small green leaves turn a brilliant golden color. The black birch is often used in landscaping, where it grows to heights of 50 feet (15 m). In the wild, it can reach up to 80 feet tall (24 m).

Eastern Hemlock The eastern hemlock is the most common evergreen tree in Connecticut. As an evergreen, its leaves do not change color or die in cooler seasons. It has thin green needles and drops many small cones. While it is a medium to large tree in the wild, some varieties have been bred to be shrubs and hedges for landscaping.

Goldenrod This small flowering plant is native to meadows and thickets, but now it can be seen along roads and highways. There are many species of goldenrod, and they can have very different appearances. Most have brilliant yellow flowers that make them quite beautiful in the spring. Goldenrods are also an important source of food for bees and butterflies.

Red Maple The red maple is the most common tree in Connecticut. About one-quarter of all trees in the state are red maples. Its leaves have a distinctive three lobes that make it easy to tell apart from other trees. In the fall, the red maple's foliage can turn a variety of colors from yellow to burgundy.

Witch Hazel This shrub is found in forests and marshes throughout Connecticut. Native Americans used it to treat many different health ailments. Now its bark and leaves are used to make shampoo, cosmetics, and skin cream. Connecticut is the main producer of this important plant.

Red maple

Witch hazel

Fauna

American Robin The state bird of Connecticut is the American robin. It is a common sight in yards and parks. The robin can be identified by its orange breast, gray back, and black head. They feed on worms and berries, and their eggs are a distinctive light-blue color that is often called "robin egg blue."

American Shad The American shad was designated the state fish of Connecticut in 2003. These small fish only grow up to 30 inches (76 cm), but they are a popular catch for fishermen in the state. Shad live most of their life in the ocean, but they swim into freshwater stream and rivers, especially the Connecticut River, to spawn.

American shad

Black Bear Black bears can grow up to 450 pounds (204 kilograms). Despite their size, they tend to run away from humans and eat mostly grasses, fruits, nuts, and berries. Black bears went extinct in Connecticut in the mid-1800s and only returned in the 1980s. Greater protection of wildlife and their forest habitat made their return possible.

Moose These massive mammals can weigh up to 1,400 pounds (635 kg). Scientists are unsure if moose lived in Connecticut before the arrival of Europeans. They typically live farther north. Early sightings occurred in the 1900s, but the animals likely lived in neighboring states most of the time. It was not until the 2000s that moose calves became a regular sight in Connecticut, and it was certain that a population had taken up residence.

Sperm Whale In 1975, the Connecticut Assembly designated the sperm whale as the state animal. Sperm whales are the largest toothed whales. They dive deep in the ocean and eat giant squid found in the depths. In Connecticut's early history, the sperm whale was central to the important whaling industry that brought money to the area.

Sperm whale

Thomas Hooker and his group of settlers reached Hartford in 1636.

2 The History of Connecticut

Throughout American history, Connecticut has played an important role. It was one of the earliest places of European settlement. Its constitution, the first of its kind, was influential in the birth of the United States. During **industrialization**, Connecticut played a leading role. Many of the innovations that drove the United States to become a world power were first used in Connecticut.

Early Colonization

In 1614, a Dutch explorer named Adriaen Block sailed up the Connecticut River almost as far as what is now Massachusetts. He found a Native American fort along the river near the area that became Hartford. More Dutch returned to Connecticut to trade with the Native Americans, but they did not settle in the area.

The English were the first Europeans to build homes and raise families along the Connecticut River. By 1630, two separate groups of English settlers had reached Massachusetts, just north of Connecticut. The Pilgrims lived in Plymouth. In Boston, people known as Puritans had just arrived. Both groups were

FAST FACT
The novel *The Last of the Mohicans* was published in 1826 and was made into a Hollywood film in 1992. The work blended the Mohegan tribe of Connecticut and the Mohican tribe of New York—two very distinct peoples. This mistake caused confusion about the two tribes for many people.

Today, a statue of Thomas Hooker stands in Hartford.

Protestants. They came to North America to practice their religion because England did not give them the freedom to worship as they chose. Besides religious freedom, this new land across the Atlantic Ocean offered settlers a chance to make new and more **prosperous** lives.

In 1631, Native Americans from the Podunk tribe located in the Connecticut region traveled to Plymouth. They invited the Pilgrims to come live and trade on their land. The Podunks also wanted English military aid to stop raids carried out by the Pequot tribe. In 1633, a small group of English traders built a trading post in what is now Windsor.

That same year, some Puritans explored the Connecticut Valley. One of them said the area had "many very desirable places ... fit to receive many hundred inhabitants." Soon, more English came to trade and farm along the Connecticut River. The largest group, Puritans led by Thomas Hooker, reached Hartford in 1636. Other Puritans went to today's Saybrook, at the mouth of the Connecticut River, and to New Haven, on Long Island Sound.

Although some Native Americans welcomed the English, others did not. The Europeans brought goods and trade items that proved useful, but they also brought diseases to which Native Americans had no resistance. As a result, many of the Native Americans died of illnesses such as smallpox.

Many English settlers also did not respect the Native Americans' ways of life and their rights to the land. Some English settlers felt that they had a claim to the land, even though the Native Americans had been living there for many years. They did not understand the religions of the Native Americans and considered them uncivilized people. While some Native

The Pequot War pitted the Pequots against English settlers and other Native American tribes.

Americans were persuaded to become Christians and adopt the ways of the Europeans, others resisted the English people's growing power.

The English settlers' relations with the Pequots were especially poor. The Pequots did not want to lose lands to the new arrivals. They stood against the English and the tribes who sided with them. In 1637, small conflicts between the Pequots and the English turned into the Pequot War. The English troops had the support of another tribe, the Mohegans, and their chief, Uncas. Together, they attacked and burned many Pequot villages.

Some historians believe that this defeat of the Pequots was a turning point for English colonization. The English gained new allies and no longer had to face this large and powerful group of Native Americans opposed to their settlements.

Native Americans in Connecticut

"Wetu" is another name for a wigwam.

This piece of pottery was made by a member of the Mohegan tribe in the 1600s.

Schemitzun, the Feast of Green Corn and Dance Powwow, is held every year in Mashantucket.

The Native Americans first arrived in the Connecticut region about ten thousand years ago. Brent Colley, a historian from Redding, has identified early paths used by Native Americans to get around the state that correspond to modern Connecticut roads such as Route 1. As many as ten thousand Native Americans may have lived in the area that became Connecticut when Europeans first arrived.

The northeast section of Connecticut and part of Massachusetts was occupied by the Nipmuc tribe. Southeastern Connecticut was occupied by the Mohegan and Pequot tribes, which were once united under the same chief. The northwest part of the state was occupied by the Mohican (or Mahican), who also lived in eastern New York. In the Southwest were the Quiripi (including the Mattabesic, Paugusett, and Schaghticoke). There were also other tribes, including the Podunk. Just before the Europeans arrived, the Pequots conquered more than half of the state. These tribes spoke a group of related languages called the Algonquian languages.

The Native people's diet was a varied one. They raised beans, squash, and corn. They also hunted, fished, and collected nuts and berries. They made their homes from trees and brush that grew in the woods. All parts of the hunted animals were used for things such as food and clothing. Many of their implements (axes, gouges, arrowheads, and knives) were made of stone. Wood was commonly used to make utensils, bowls, and pipes with beautiful carvings on them. Containers were made from tree bark.

The most common shelter built by Native Americans was a wigwam, which was generally dome-shaped. The men would collect saplings and place them upright in a circle on the ground. The saplings were bent and tied together, then covered with bark or woven mats, depending on the weather. A hole was cut in the top to allow campfire smoke to escape. The entrance was made from the skin of an animal hung over an opening.

Epidemics and warfare nearly wiped out the Native American tribes in Connecticut, so they had to merge to survive. All their languages were lost. Many were driven from their lands, although some, such as the Pequots, were allowed to return to reservations close to their original homes.

Today there are two federally recognized tribes in Connecticut: the Mashantucket Pequot Tribe and the Mohegan Tribe. In addition, the state recognizes three more tribes: the Eastern Pequot Tribal Nation, the Golden Hill Paugussett, and the Schaghticoke Tribal Nation.

The Mohegans

In the early 1600s, the Mohegan tribe split with the Pequots after disagreeing about how to handle the European settlers. The Mohegans favored collaboration with the English and joined them to fight the Pequots. The Mohegans helped the English defeat the Pequots in 1637, which helped keep Mohegans relatively safe during later wars.

Clothing: Clothing was fashioned from fur and leather, as well as from twined materials, often insulated with feathers. Twining is a weaving technique where two weft strands are wrapped and twisted around a warp strand.

Art: Mohegans were known for making mats and baskets. Dolls made of household items were used to remind children that nothing should be wasted.

Gender Roles: Female Mohegan members traditionally worked in the fields, prepared food, and cared for children, while men hunted and protected the tribe. However, women often held positions of great responsibility. Women traditionally chose tribal leaders.

Today: For over 350 years, treaties and laws have highlighted the tribe's independent status. The US federal government formally recognized the Mohegan Nation on March 7, 1994. Today, the Mohegan Nation controls its own government and lands. After the passage of the Indian Gaming Regulatory Act (IGRA) in 1988, the Mohegans successfully built the Mohegan Sun Casino, which shares tens of millions of dollars of revenue with Connecticut each year. Connecticut's Native American tribes are thus one of the state's most significant sources of income.

Connecticut Colony

In 1639, the Hartford settlement drafted rules for forming its own government. Thomas Hooker told the settlers, "The foundation of authority is … in the free consent of the people." The settlers would elect people to represent their common interests, much as in Massachusetts. However, the Connecticut settlers were the first Americans to write down the rules for their government, called the Fundamental Orders. The rules for forming a government can also be called a constitution. Because of the importance of the Fundamental Orders, Connecticut is known as the Constitution State.

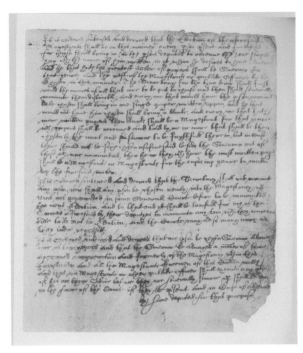

Connecticut settlers wrote their own rules in a document called the Fundamental Orders.

Although the English settlers in Connecticut now had their own government, they were still tied to England, their home country. In 1662, Connecticut received a charter from England. This legal document made the different settlements in Connecticut part of one colony. The charter also allowed the residents to keep the government they had already formed.

Most English settlers in Connecticut were farmers. They belonged to the Congregational Church, which was the church of the Puritans. Even though the Puritans left England in part for religious freedom, the settlers decided that only members of this church could freely practice their religion in the colony. This limit on religious freedom kept other Europeans from coming to Connecticut.

After another war between colonists and Native American tribes in 1676, known as King Philip's War, Connecticut became mostly peaceful for the English settlers. However, the Native Americans were almost wiped out. Many died from illnesses the English brought with them. Others had died in the wars or had left the region when they lost their lands.

The population of settlers grew rapidly during the 1700s. Farmers raised crops such as corn, rye, and barley. Some residents worked building ships, while others made iron or ground wheat into flour at mills set up along rivers. Many Connecticut men and women ran shops, taverns, and inns. In New Haven, students attended one of America's first educational institutions, Yale College, now known as Yale University.

The American Revolution

By the mid-1770s, many Americans were calling for independence from England, now a part of Great Britain. In Connecticut, many people supported the call for freedom, but others wanted to remain part of Great Britain.

When the American Revolution began in 1775, Connecticut played an important role. Its early military heroes included General Israel Putnam. At the Battle of Bunker Hill in Boston, Putnam is said to have given the famous order, "Don't fire until you see the whites of their eyes."

Another Connecticut hero was Nathan Hale, a schoolteacher turned soldier. He served as an American spy during the war until the British caught and hanged him.

FAST FACT

Connecticut has provided supplies for America's army throughout history. In the Revolutionary War, it was called "The **Provision** State" due to the ammunition, food, and clothes it gave to George Washington's army. It did the same during both world wars and later built many submarines for the US Navy. Today, it is still a leader of the defense industry.

General Israel Putnam led soldiers during the American Revolution.

Whaling was an important industry in Connecticut until the late 1800s. Sailors killed the massive creatures for their meat, blubber, teeth, bones, and spermaceti. Spermaceti is a waxy substance that gives sperm whales their name. It was used to make candles and cosmetics at the time.

Before he died, Hale said, "I only regret that I have but one life to lose for my country."

The American Revolution ended in 1783. Connecticut had helped win the revolution in many important ways, including supplying guns, cannons, and other items to the troops. In 1788, five years after the war ended, Connecticut became the fifth state to ratify the new US Constitution.

The Growth of Industry

By the nineteenth century, Connecticut had little farmland left for new settlers. It was also hard for farmers already there to make a living. Its rocky landscape and small size meant that Connecticut had less fertile land than other states, making it difficult to compete in farming.

Over time, manufacturing and trade replaced farming as the center of economic activity. Cities gained fame for making different products. Waterbury became known as the "Brass City," and Meriden became the "Silver City." Plymouth made clocks. Danbury made headwear and became "Hat City." Banks and insurance companies grew in Hartford, the "Insurance Capital." Shipbuilding remained important along the Connecticut River and Long Island Sound. New London became the center of Connecticut's whaling trade.

In the nineteenth century, Connecticut was an important center of the North American whaling industry.

One newspaper writer in the mid-1800s was impressed with the number of talented people who came from the state. "Everybody worth knowing was born in Connecticut—or should have been," the journalist wrote. "It is the most extraordinary patch of land in the known world."

Traders from Connecticut traveled all over the country selling goods made in the state. These people were often called Yankee peddlers. The peddlers sold many items, including nutmeg, a spice from the seed produced by the nutmeg tree. Nutmeg is often used in pies, puddings, cakes, and cookies. Due to the spice's popularity, Connecticut is often nicknamed the Nutmeg State, and its people are called Nutmeggers.

Connecticut peddlers were well known for selling nutmeg seeds.

Innovation

Connecticut inventors played a large role in building the state's economy. In 1836, Hartford-born Samuel Colt patented a new kind of pistol. The Colt revolver was the first firearm that could shoot five or six bullets without reloading. Before Colt's invention, only one- or two-barrel flintlock pistols were available. Colt later built a huge factory in Hartford.

Connecticut also became a leader in producing machines and tools that made other items. In 1793, a Yale graduate named Eli Whitney invented the cotton gin (short for "engine"), a machine that separates cotton fibers from seeds. Whitney then developed the idea of mass production—a faster, less expensive way to manufacture goods. Before this innovation, products such as guns were made one at a time, by hand. It took a lot of time to make each gun, and it was difficult to find replacement parts. Whitney came up with a plan to build milling machines that could easily make many identical copies of each gun part. Workers would then assemble the parts quickly and cheaply, making many guns that were exactly the same.

Eli Whitney's cotton gin changed America's economy.

Whitney opened a factory in New Haven, and his ideas for mass production spread to other factories throughout the state. Through the nineteenth century, some notable products made in Connecticut included typewriters, bicycles, sewing machines, and textiles for clothing.

Slavery and the Civil War

While Connecticut was changing, so was the nation. Tensions stemming from differences between the Northern states and Southern states were rising. The North and the South had different economies. The Southern states depended on slavery to keep their **agricultural** economy going. The Northern states had more industry and did not have the same need for slaves. Some Northerners also believed that human slavery was wrong in a free society.

Like most Northern states, Connecticut itself had a mixed past when it came to the

Slaves in the South worked on farms called plantations.

issue of slavery. Not many slaves lived in the colony in the early 1700s. However, by the start of the American Revolution, Connecticut had the largest number of slaves in New England, although its total number of slaves (about 6,500) was much smaller than in the Southern states. Runaway slaves in Connecticut were always **prosecuted** and returned to their masters. The Connecticut legislature rejected bills to free slaves three times—in 1777, 1779, and 1780. Even free blacks in Connecticut suffered from discrimination.

During these years, there were groups in the state that worked tirelessly to end slavery. While some Northern states abolished the practice altogether, others, including Connecticut, enacted laws to gradually free individuals held in slavery. Connecticut passed a gradual **emancipation** act in 1784. Slavery was finally abolished in the state in 1848.

Even while slavery was still legal in Connecticut, some people worked to help escaped slaves find freedom. From the 1830s until the end of the Civil War, the Underground Railroad helped slaves from the South reach freedom in slavery-free states. The Underground Railroad was a network that consisted of white **abolitionists**, free blacks, and escaped slaves.

Conductors—the people who would lead the escaped slaves north to freedom—met the slaves at a designated point in the South and led them north at night. Others gave the conductors and slaves shelter and food. Researchers have identified many buildings in Connecticut as stops along the Underground Railroad. These sites are honored as part of the Connecticut Freedom Trail.

The story of the *Amistad* also shows how Connecticut played a part in the fight against slavery. In 1839, a group of African slaves revolted

The Greater Hartford Festival of Jazz

Each year in Hartford, people gather to attend a massive, free jazz festival in Bushnell Park. The event lasts for days, and attendees can listen to some of the best jazz musicians in the world. The Greater Hartford Festival of Jazz began in 1992. Before that, Hartford local and bass player Paul Brown had been organizing jazz performances in Bushnell Park for decades.

Bushnell Park is the oldest publicly funded park in the United States. Its beautiful setting and large pavilion are perfect for the festival and spotlight Connecticut's long history. The park is even home to a descendent of the famous Charter Oak called the Footguard Oak that was planted in 1871.

The festival is the largest free jazz festival in New England. In 2017, more than seventy thousand people attended. Performers have included some of the

The Greater Hartford Festival of Jazz is New England's biggest free jazz festival.

most famous names in jazz, like the legendary Dave Brubeck, who appeared on the cover of *Time* magazine, and McCoy Tyner.

The festival is supported entirely by donations. Local businesses and individuals donate to keep the festival free of charge and open to anyone who wants to enjoy good music and days of entertainment.

against their captors on the slave transport ship *Amistad*. The vessel eventually arrived in New London. The Africans spent more than a year in jail in New Haven, hoping to win their freedom in court. With the legal help of former US president John Quincy Adams,

Artist Hale Woodruff painting his *Amistad Murals*

the Africans eventually won their freedom and were allowed to go back to their homelands.

Before leaving the United States, they spent almost a year in Farmington, where the local residents housed, clothed, and educated them. People of Connecticut also helped raise money for the Africans' journey back home. The incident has been called the most important battle for civil rights in Connecticut and may have helped the state to finally abolish slavery in 1848.

The Civil War was fought from 1861 to 1865. It pitted the Union, or Northern states, against the proslavery Confederacy in the South. Connecticut sent more than fifty thousand men to fight for the Union. Soldiers from Connecticut included an African American military unit called the Connecticut Twenty-Ninth Colored Regiment. Connecticut also supported the war effort by providing weapons, clothing, and food to the Union soldiers.

The World Wars

Life in Connecticut changed after the South was defeated and the Civil War ended. By 1910, most Nutmeggers lived in cities and towns instead of on farms. Farmland was better and more plentiful

This map shows the Confederacy in red and the Union in blue. Light blue states were part of the Union but allowed slavery. States in white weren't yet part of the United States.

The 303rd Machine Gun Battalion marches in a Hartford parade during World War I.

in the Midwest and West, so industry became the major source of jobs in Connecticut. More and more Nutmeggers started to work in factories.

During World War I, which lasted from 1914 to 1918, the state produced guns and other weapons. After the United States entered the war in 1917, Connecticut once again provided the nation with brave men and women who served in or worked for the military.

World War II (1939–1945) brought even more changes. Supplying engines and other parts for airplanes became the state's major industry even before the United States entered the fight in 1941. Across Connecticut, women went to work in the factories to provide supplies and equipment during the war while men fought overseas.

Connecticut's African American population also continued to grow. People of color had lived in Connecticut since colonial times, both as free people and as slaves. During World War II, Northern factories needed workers, so many African Americans from the South headed to Connecticut for jobs, increasing the African American population even further.

The Modern Era

Many manufacturing companies and other businesses have moved out of the state since World War II. Companies in the service industry grew to take their place. Banks, government agencies, and schools all expanded. Companies providing services to tourists also grew.

New businesses continue to create jobs in Connecticut. Insurance companies have

Greenhouses are very important in Connecticut. Farmers grow all sorts of plants in them both for food and decoration. The glass or plastic of the greenhouse traps sunlight in the space and keeps the plants warm. Using everyday objects, you can make your own terrarium at home that does the same thing!

Make Your Own Terrarium

Supplies

- Scissors
- Dirt (from a store or the outdoors)
- Plant (you can dig one up, careful to not damage its roots, or buy one at a garden store)
- Two-liter bottle
- Tape

Directions

1. First, stand the bottle up and measure about 4 inches (10 cm) from the bottom. Ask an adult to cut the bottle here so that the bottom third of the bottle is now open on top.

2. Add your dirt to this base. Place your plant in the dirt and make sure its roots are covered. If you bought a plant from a garden store, do not remove the dirt from the bottom.

3. Tape the top of the bottle back into place to form your terrarium.

4. When the soil is very dry, you can water the plant by unscrewing the cap. The bottle will keep the plant warm and moist just like a greenhouse!

This greenhouse is in Hamden. You can make a terrarium that works like a greenhouse.

Stamford has become an entertainment and media hub.

expanded, and the state has become a major center for scientific and medical research. The Stamford area in particular has seen an increase in companies involved with entertainment and media. Cable sports network ESPN's headquarters and main facilities are located in Bristol, Connecticut, where the company employs more than four thousand people.

In 1983, the Mashantucket Pequot Tribal Nation was recognized by the federal government. The government acknowledged their claim to a tract of land in Connecticut, and they were given ownership of it. Just three years later, the tribe opened a casino to bring money into the community. The Foxwoods Resort Casino grew into the largest casino in the United States. It now has more than ten thousand employees. These jobs are vital to the economy of Connecticut. Additionally, the casino brings many tourists into the state. These visitors then spend money outside the casino, bringing even more money into the state's economy.

The Mohegan Tribe followed suit in 1996 and opened their own casino in Uncasville, Connecticut. Called Mohegan Sun, it also grew to be a major source of jobs and money in the state. The two casinos helped fuel the expansion of the services industry in the state. They also pay 25 percent of their slot machine winnings to the state government of Connecticut.

This money is needed to keep the state deficit under control. A deficit occurs when more money is spent than earned. Many states have a

budget deficit. Deficits result in debt over time, as money is borrowed for spending. While nearly all governments, both national and local, have some debt, too much debt is a bad thing. It costs some money each year to have debt. In 2017, Connecticut was estimated to owe $22,745 for each person in the state. Only New Jersey owed more money per resident. Part of this was public debt, but part of it was also due to pensions.

Foxwoods Resort Casino is part of the Mashantucket reservation.

Pensions are money that is promised to retired employees, often teachers, police officers, and firefighters. States have a responsibility to pay these promised pensions, but they must use tax money to do so. Connecticut's current debt and pension problems are being dealt with by the state government. In 2016, George Mason University's Mercatus Center ranked Connecticut as the worst state when it came to its deficit and debt. The next year, Connecticut had risen from number fifty to number thirty-seven, though there is still a great deal of work to be done.

Important People from Connecticut

Marian Anderson

Born in 1897, Marian Anderson went on to become one of the most famous singers of her generation. She performed around the world but was turned away from some events in the United States because she was black. Anderson was active in the civil rights movement and fought for the rights of all African Americans. After traveling the world, she lived much of her later life on a farm in Danbury, Connecticut.

Marian Anderson

Benedict Arnold

The military officer Benedict Arnold was born in Norwich when Connecticut was still a British colony. During the Revolutionary War, he governed the important city of Philadelphia for George Washington before changing sides and fighting for the British. His betrayal led to his name becoming a word for traitor. After the war, he never again returned to the newly independent United States.

Prudence Crandall

Now the state heroine of Connecticut, Prudence Crandall was once imprisoned by the state for running a school for African American girls. During the 1830s, schooling African American girls was hugely unpopular, but Crandall took a stand against bigotry and racism. Even after being briefly imprisoned, she refused to close the school until a mob attacked it. Fearing for the safety of her students, she finally closed the school but continued to fight injustice.

Nathan Hale

Nathan Hale

Nathan Hale was a just nineteen years old when the Revolutionary War broke out in 1775. Nonetheless, the Yale College graduate joined the independence struggle and volunteered to spy on British troops. After being discovered by the British, he famously said, "I only regret that I have but one life to lose for my country."

Thomas Hooker

The man known as the "father of Connecticut" founded one of the first major settlements in the colony in 1636. He was a respected leader of the Puritans, a Christian group who founded Boston as well. He had strong beliefs that people ought to govern themselves and be able to vote. These ideas helped shape Connecticut's history and early laws.

Helen Keller

Helen Keller was a famous American writer, lecturer, and activist. After losing her sight and hearing as a small child, she learned to communicate through sign language and eventually graduated from college. At the time, this kind of achievement was unheard of. Keller spent the last two decades of her life in Easton, Connecticut.

Helen Keller

James William Charles Pennington

This famous intellectual was born into slavery in Maryland before escaping and moving north. He was the first African American to attend Yale University, although he was not allowed to speak in class or officially enroll. James W. C. Pennington spoke out about injustices like these and slavery across New England.

Harriet Beecher Stowe

Connecticut native Harriet Beecher Stowe was an author and abolitionist. Her most famous work is *Uncle Tom's Cabin*, which portrayed the horrors and violence of slavery. It was published shortly before the Civil War and stoked tensions over slavery. Stowe was born in Litchfield, Connecticut, and passed away in Hartford, but she spent a great deal of time outside the state in Ohio and Florida.

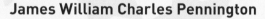

Nutmeggers celebrate the two-hundredth anniversary of the War of 1812.

3 Who Lives in Connecticut?

Connecticut is home to more than three and a half million Americans. During colonial times, nearly its entire population was from England. In the 1800s, people from other European countries migrated to Connecticut. Over the past century, many African Americans, Hispanics, and Asian immigrants have made the state their home. As a result, Connecticut is home to a **diverse** population that is united by their love of the Constitution State.

Religious Diversity

The people of Connecticut practice many different religions. The largest group is Roman Catholic. Many others belong to various Protestant churches, including Congregational, Episcopal, Lutheran, Methodist, and Baptist.

Jewish settlers first came to Connecticut in the 1700s. Recently, Russian Jewish immigrants have come to the state. Newer immigrants from Asia practice religions such as Islam, Buddhism, and Hinduism.

FAST FACT

The Mohegan and Pequot people still live in Connecticut. However, the last speaker of the Mohegan Pequot language, Fidelia Fielding, died in 1908. In recent years, the tribes and academics have worked together to revive this language. Resources to learn it are now available online.

Followers of Judaism first arrived in Connecticut in the 1700s. This photo shows Beth Hamedrash Hagodol synagogue in Hartford.

The people from these different cultures and religions have helped to shape Connecticut into the culturally diverse state it is today.

Native Americans

In 1980, only about four thousand residents in Connecticut considered themselves Native Americans. This grew to about thirty-one thousand people in the 2010 census. Most of this growth came when the Mashantucket Pequot and the Mohegan tribal nations received federal recognition from the US government. This recognition means that the tribes can run their lands as separate nations.

Many members of these tribes had left Connecticut in the past but have since returned. They can now share their heritage while living on their tribal lands. Denise Porter, a Pequot who returned, said, "I felt that [the tribal nation] was part of me. I thought, 'This is good, because I'm back home and I'm working for my own people.'"

With federal recognition, they can also run businesses of their choice. The Pequots and Mohegans have used their tribal land to build casinos, earning hundreds of

FAST FACT

Immigrants born in other countries make up 14 percent of Connecticut's population. The largest number come from Jamaica, India, Mexico, China, and Poland. Immigrants are more likely to start small businesses than those born in the United States. They account for nearly 24 percent of self-employed people in the state.

The Mashantucket Pequot Museum and Research Center celebrates Pequot heritage.

millions of dollars for themselves and the state. Some of their money goes toward maintaining their lands and businesses and funding education for their young people.

Many Native Americans also want to share their history and culture with others. The Mashantucket Pequots have established the Mashantucket Pequot Museum and Research Center. It includes full-size exhibits of Pequot farmers and hunters and shows details of life from the past and present.

Some Native American groups stayed in Connecticut even after they lost their traditional lands. The Schaghticoke Reservation can be found in Litchfield County, along the border between Connecticut and New York. The Eastern Pequot Reservation is in North Stonington. These groups are proud of their heritage and often travel to schools and events across Connecticut to teach others. Many of these tribes, including the Schaghticokes and the Eastern Pequots, are still seeking recognition for their tribes from the US government.

Spreading Suburbs

Most Connecticut residents live in cities or suburbs. The state's largest cities are Bridgeport, New Haven, Stamford, and Hartford. Except for Stamford, the population of all these cities decreased during the 1990s. Some residents moved to find better or different jobs, or to raise their families in the quieter suburbs.

Stratford is one of Connecticut's thriving suburbs.

Hartford had the largest drop in population, as more than eighteen thousand people moved out. In 2001, in an effort to bring new life to the capital city, Hartford broke ground on a building project called Adriaen's Landing. Today, the site includes a convention center, a four-star hotel, and a state-of-the-art science center.

Income and Education

As Connecticut's population changes, the state faces a growing problem. Many people have good jobs and live well, particularly in some of the suburbs. For example, the average family income is well over $200,000 in New Canaan and Darien in Fairfield County. This area near Long Island Sound is sometimes called the Gold Coast and includes some of the wealthiest areas in the United States.

Areas like these sometime lead people to assume that everyone in Connecticut is wealthy, but not all the towns and cities are as prosperous. In truth, Connecticut has a large gap between its rich and poor. Many people have trouble finding good jobs. For example, Hartford's income has fallen recently, and more than 30 percent of its people now live in poverty. Families in other cities and towns have also seen their income drop.

This gulf between rich and poor is obvious in some of Connecticut's schools. The state boasts several of the nation's top private schools, while many of its cities and towns also have highly regarded public schools. Connecticut also contains many highly ranked colleges and universities, including famous private institutions as well as a well-respected state university system, which includes the University of Connecticut.

However, some of Connecticut's public schools sit at the other end of the spectrum. This difference was brought to the public's attention in 1989 when Milo Sheff, a student at a Hartford elementary school, sued the state. He claimed he was being denied equal education, arguing that minority children in cities like Hartford did not get the same quality of education as schoolchildren in some suburbs and smaller towns. Sheff and the others wanted the state to provide equal education for all students,

Bridgeport leaders are working to revive the city's economy.

Connecticut has worked hard to offer high-quality public schools.

1. University of Connecticut, Storrs

(19,241 undergraduate students)

2. Central Connecticut State University, New Britain

(9,554 undergraduate students)

3. Post University, Waterbury

(7,844 undergraduate students)

4. Quinnipiac University, Hamden

(7,361 undergraduate students)

5. Yale University, New Haven

(5,746 undergraduate students)

6. Sacred Heart University, Fairfield

(5,603 undergraduate students)

7. University of New Haven

(5,216 undergraduate students)

8. Western Connecticut State University, Danbury

(5,082 undergraduate students)

9. Eastern Connecticut State University, Willimantic

(5,073 undergraduate students)

10. University of Hartford, West Hartford

(5,069 undergraduate students)

Connecticut's Biggest Colleges and Universities

(Enrollment numbers are from *US News and World Report* 2019 college rankings.)

University of Connecticut

Central Connecticut State University

Yale University

Changing Demographics

Connecticut's modern-day diversity resulted from many different waves of immigration. While the first Europeans to arrive were Dutch, they were soon outnumbered by English settlers. During the colonial era, nearly all residents of Connecticut were from England. By 1790, people of English ancestry made up approximately 96 percent of the population. African Americans accounted for just 2 percent. But during the 1800s, a new wave of European immigration changed Connecticut's population.

Economic turmoil and wars in Europe drove many people to leave the continent and seek a new start in the United States. Some of these people came to Connecticut to work in new factories opening in the state. The first group to arrive in large numbers were the Irish. By the 1820s, they made up more than one-third of new arrivals to Connecticut. Later in the 1800s, many people from Italy, Poland, and Austria-Hungary also immigrated to Connecticut. The state that was once nearly entirely English had become quite diverse. Many different languages could be heard in cities around the state.

This 1891 illustration shows a Hartford factory. Many immigrants found work in Connecticut's factories in the 1800s.

By the early 1900s, Connecticut had become a state of people who had been born across the ocean. In 1914, just 35 percent of the people living in Connecticut had been born in the United States! A diverse mix of mostly European immigrants called the state home. They kept many of their customs and traditions from home, but they tended to be fiercely proud of their new homeland.

In the twentieth century, Connecticut's demographics changed once more. African Americans from the South moved north in large numbers. They were fleeing persecution in the South as well as looking for jobs that the North provided. Immigrants from around the world, including Asia and Latin America, also began to arrive in large numbers for the first time. Today, these people of non-European descent make up approximately one-quarter of the state's population.

Nutmeggers enjoy the Little Poland Festival in New Britain.

Connecticut's history of immigration can still be felt in the present day. Immigrants continue to seek opportunities in the state. Communities that have been here for generations still celebrate their background and speak languages from around the world. This is easy to see in the city of New Britain—also called "Little Poland." Polish shops and restaurants line the streets there. Visitors can even buy newspapers published in Polish. Each year, tens of thousands of people attend the New Britain Little Poland Festival to celebrate the community's heritage. Connecticut's diversity is still a source of pride and strength for the state.

regardless of where they lived. The case, known as *Sheff v. O'Neill*, went all the way to Connecticut's Supreme Court. In 1996, the court finally ruled that the state had an obligation to make sure that all Connecticut children have access to equal levels and standards of education.

Since the 1996 decision, Sheff plaintiffs have been working with Hartford public schools, the city of Hartford, and the state of Connecticut to create programs that try to eliminate racial isolation in schools. These efforts have resulted in substantial gains.

More than 1,600 Hartford students now take part in Open Choice, a program that allows urban students to attend public schools in nearby suburban towns, or suburban and rural students to attend public schools in a nearby urban center. Students can also attend regional magnet schools, where they come together to learn in educational settings that offer a range of themes or teaching philosophies.

Connecticut's Appeal

Connecticut offers many reasons for people to live in the state. Some residents like the state's location. It is close to two major cities, New York and Boston, but it also has plenty of woodlands and open spaces. For people who enjoy boating, rivers and lakes abound, and Long Island Sound is nearby. Some of New England's best mountains for skiing are also close to Connecticut.

Connecticut's largest businesses provide good jobs. Connecticut has highly educated workers skilled in such areas as computers, engineering, and insurance. The state's hospitals do important medical research. Overall, many of Connecticut's schools are among the best in the nation.

The state's cities offer plenty of art and entertainment. Hartford's Wadsworth Atheneum,

George W. Bush

On July 6, 1946, George W. Bush was born in New Haven. His father, George H. W. Bush, soon moved the family to Texas, but the younger Bush returned to the state to attend Yale University. In 2000, George W. Bush was elected president of the United States. He served for two terms.

John Mayer

Born in Bridgeport, John Mayer began playing the guitar at thirteen years old. He briefly attended Berklee College of Music in nearby Boston, but soon dropped out. Just a few years later, he released his hit album *Room for Squares*. Since then, the singer-songwriter has won seven Grammy Awards.

Stephanie McMahon

Hartford native Stephanie McMahon rose to the top of the male-dominated professional wrestling world. The daughter of legendary wrestler promoter Vince McMahon, she is now a top executive of the WWE (World Wrestling Entertainment, Inc.). She has also appeared in the ring and wrestled with a number of other pro wrestlers.

Evan Ross

Evan Ross was born in Greenwich. His mother is the famous lead singer of the Supremes, Diana Ross. As a teenager, Evan Ross began working as an actor and appeared in the HBO drama *Life Support*. He appeared in the final two *Hunger Games* movies, and in 2014 he married fellow celebrity Ashlee Simpson.

Meg Ryan

Actress Meg Ryan was born in Fairfield in 1961. She began appearing in a soap opera in 1982 but was catapulted to stardom in 1986 when she had a role in the hit movie *Top Gun*. Ryan went on to star in many romantic comedies, including *When Harry Met Sally*.

Celebrities from Connecticut

John Mayer

Stephanie McMahon

Evan Ross

Make Your Own Lollipops

In 1908, George Smith of New Haven, Connecticut, began selling hard candy on a stick to make it easier to eat. He trademarked the name Lolly Pop for his creation, and the candy soon grew in popularity. You can make your own lollipops at home with just a few ingredients.

Ingredients

- 1 cup of sugar
- $1/3$ cup of water
- $1/3$ cup of light corn syrup
- Food coloring
- Lollipop sticks
- Candy thermometer
- Parchment paper

Directions

1. Prepare a baking sheet by covering it in parchment paper. This keeps the lollipops from sticking or making a mess. Place the lollipop sticks about two inches apart on the parchment paper.
2. Combine the sugar, water, and corn syrup in a small saucepan. Put the saucepan on the stove on medium-high.
3. Use a candy thermometer to check the temperature. When it reaches 305 degrees Fahrenheit, take the saucepan off the stove.
4. Wait until it stops bubbling and mix in food coloring until the color looks the way you want it to.
5. Carefully spoon the mixture onto the ends of the sticks. You can make whatever shape you want.
6. Let the lollipops cool for about 30 minutes until they are hard. Now they are ready to enjoy!

the oldest public art museum in the United States, owns about fifty thousand pieces of art from around the world. Bridgeport is home to the state's only zoo, the Beardsley. Its New World Tropics Building features animals from the rain forests of South America.

In New Haven, Yale University's Peabody Museum displays some of the first dinosaur bones found in North America. Each June, the city sponsors the International Festival of Arts and Ideas. Performers entertain on city streets and in theaters across New Haven. The state also has amusement parks, shopping malls, and other places that are perfect for relaxing and having fun.

Currently, one of the biggest issues facing Connecticut is the number of people living there. Its population is growing very slowly—it ranks among the five slowest-growing states. Slow population growth can be a problem when it affects the economy.

Luckily, Connecticut's attractions, jobs, and location are helping to draw new residents to the state. Population growth is largely driven by immigration to the state and minority communities. Hispanics and Latinos make up more than half of the total population growth in Connecticut.

Wadsworth Atheneum

Pratt Street Historic District in Hartford

This manufacturing plant in Torrington makes clean energy products that provide power without using nonrenewable resources.

4 At Work in Connecticut

W orkers in Connecticut have jobs in many different industries. From agriculture to manufacturing, many products are still made in the state. People are needed to drive this production, even when factories are **automated**. The services sector is also strong. This includes all businesses that offer a service rather than make a product, from stores and banks to software companies. People looking for a job in Connecticut can find many different opportunities to choose from.

Agriculture

While agriculture no longer holds its once-prominent position in Connecticut's economy, farming is still important. Connecticut farmers produce nearly $600 million worth of agricultural products each year. However, sometimes it costs too much to run a farm. An easier way for farmers to make money is to sell their farms to corporations that would like to develop—or build on—their land. Connecticut loses some farmland each year to development.

FAST FACT

Connecticut's small size and its location between New York and Boston mean that many people leave the state to work. They drive or take the train every day to work out of state. This can lead to long commutes for workers. However, Hartford ranks as one of the best cities in the country for commute times—the average is just twenty-two minutes.

Peaches are an important Connecticut crop.

A state program called the Farmland Preservation Program gives farmers money, so they can keep working their land instead of selling it to developers who build houses, stores, or offices. Through 2015, the program has protected 315 farms.

Manufacturing

Connecticut has lost many manufacturing jobs in recent years. Some companies moved out of state. Others that used to work for the US military received fewer orders to make goods, so the companies had to lay off workers.

However, manufacturers in Connecticut still make many things, and about one out of every ten residents still work in this field. The state's largest manufacturing companies build advanced products like aircraft engines, helicopters, and submarines for aircraft companies and the military. Other companies

FAST FACT

Nearly 15 percent of Connecticut's land is used for agriculture. The top sellers are nursery and greenhouse products. Ornamental shrubs and flowers, as well as Christmas trees, fall into this category. Greenhouses allow plants to grow even in Connecticut's cold climate. Other important crops are fruits like apples and peaches, as well as tobacco.

Kaman Aerosystems makes helicopters and other aircraft. The company is headquartered in Bloomfield.

are involved in metalworking, electronics, and plastics. Producing all these things requires skilled workers. Connecticut is known for its well-trained machinists and engineers.

Connecticut is also the home to many interesting—and fun—products. Connecticut is the birthplace of the Wiffle ball. The plastic bats and balls are still made in the state. Another Connecticut product is PEZ. Since 1972, all PEZ candy eaten in the United States has been produced in a factory in Orange, Connecticut.

The Tech Industry

Connecticut companies of all sizes also use science and computers to create more advanced products. Small computer software businesses have been coming to the state. Other state companies are involved with the internet and making computer parts.

One teenage Connecticut inventor turned to science to create an important new product that has improved people's health. In 2001, Michael Nyberg of Old Lyme found that certain high sounds can kill mosquitoes before they become adults. The adult mosquitoes bite people and sometimes carry deadly diseases, such as West Nile virus. "I knew I wanted to do a project in acoustics [sound]," Nyberg said. "We had this big West Nile scare, and I … kind of put the two together." For a science project, Nyberg built a device, now called the Larvasonic, to test his idea about using sound to kill the mosquitoes. The machine worked! Now, Nyberg and his family run a company to sell the machines.

Yale New Haven Hospital is part of the Yale New Haven Health System, the state's biggest employer.

The Service Sector

More than 120,000 Nutmeggers work in a group of industries sometimes called FIRE: finance, insurance, and real estate. In Connecticut, insurance and finance stand out as major industries.

The state's first insurance company opened in Hartford in 1810. Hartford continues as an important insurance center today. Stamford has grown as a **financial** and media center, in part because it is so close to New York City, with easy access by car and train. Many financial companies based in New York have offices in the Stamford area, and some companies have even moved their headquarters from New York City to Stamford.

Companies involved in FIRE are sometimes called service industries. Other service jobs include selling goods in stores, providing legal services and medical care, and working for schools. Government is also a big employer in Connecticut. About sixty thousand people work for state and local governments.

Tourism

Tourism is one part of the service industry that has grown in Connecticut. People from around the country—and around the world—like to visit Connecticut for several reasons. In the fall, many visitors come to parts of the state to admire the beautiful scenery and the colorful foliage. People visit the state during other parts

FAST FACT

Yale New Haven Health System is the state's largest employer, with more than twenty-two thousand workers. It operates five hospitals across the state and is affiliated with Yale University. Health care is a fast-growing industry both in Connecticut and across the United States.

In 2011, Governor Dannel P. Malloy announced the "Bioscience Connecticut" initiative. The state earmarked $900 million to jumpstart the bioscience industry in the state. Bioscience uses living organisms to make new products. It includes new fields of medicine that use the genes in our body, among other things, to fight disease. The field is poised to revolutionize modern medicine. Researchers hope it may hold the key to new treatments for diseases like cancer.

Connecticut has positioned itself to be a leader in the field. Drawn by the highly educated workforce and world-class universities, bioscience companies are moving to the state. In just one example, the company Sema4 announced in April of 2018 that it was moving laboratories from New York to Connecticut. The move was expected to bring 405 new jobs with it over five years.

Medicine for the Future

Bioscience opportunities are on the rise in Connecticut.

Bioscience workers tend to be highly paid. In 2016, a study found that the average salary in the field in Connecticut was $85,000. Growth in bioscience brings more money into the state. As the field continues to expand, Connecticut's economy is ready to grow as well.

Ski Sundown is one of four ski resorts in Connecticut.

of the year, looking to relax in the peace and quiet of Connecticut's countryside, participate in winter sports, or take a summer swim. They might also want to visit historic spots, such as the Mystic Seaport restored whaling village and Connecticut Freedom Trail sites honoring the state's African American heritage.

The state's cities also have a lot to offer tourists, including museums and fine restaurants. Many Nutmeggers work in the theaters, museums, and stores that tourists often visit. Whatever their reasons, and whichever part of the state tourists visit, they will need to stay and eat at Connecticut's hotels and restaurants. Not only do these businesses bring money into the state, but they also provide jobs for many Nutmeggers.

One of Connecticut's best-known businesses is ESPN (Entertainment and Sports Programming Network). It is one that residents of the state are quite proud of. ESPN was first imagined as a broadcaster of local sports games in Connecticut. The former spokesman for the Whalers hockey team, Bill Rasmussen, hoped to let local fans enjoy their games. However, he decided to expand the venture, and he bought a TV channel to broadcast to the whole country.

ESPN: "The Worldwide Leader in Sports"

In 1979, Rasmussen launched the first daily sports news program, *Sports Center*. He bought some land in Bristol, Connecticut, and built a headquarters for the new station. Over time, ESPN grew into a titan of the cable television industry. It is now owned by ABC Inc., part of the Walt Disney Company, and has many sister networks that broadcast in the United States and around the world.

Sports Center has been on the air since 1979. Here, anchors present sports news on the show in 1992.

Today, ESPN's headquarters in Bristol employs about four thousand people. It is an important part of Connecticut's economy. The company has also expanded around the country. A further four thousand people work for ESPN in other states and countries. In the spring of 2018, it opened a major new office in nearby New York City, but its headquarters remains in Bristol, where it all began.

ESPN headquarters
in Bristol

Looking to the Future

The economy across the United States began to suffer in 2008, and the downturn lasted until 2010. As the country entered a severe **recession**, workers in Connecticut felt the effects, and more than 119,000 Nutmeggers lost their jobs. In the following years, recovery was slow. Between 2010 and 2013, Connecticut only recovered about half of the jobs that were lost.

Among all US states, Connecticut still has one of the highest percentages of residents who are college graduates. These educated workers will continue to make useful new products and start new companies. American ingenuity is still strong in Connecticut. Nutmeggers from all walks of life and all different fields will work together to help their state continue to grow and move into the future.

One source of growth in Connecticut is the digital media sector. When Connecticut's economy shifted from manufacturing to services, media companies like ESPN led the way. In 2007, there was a great deal of talk about Connecticut becoming "Hollywood East." It was hoped that the state would become the media hub of the East Coast and one day compare to Hollywood in California.

While the state has not been able to compete with Hollywood for blockbuster films, it has done very well in other areas. Numerous sports broadcasters are based in Connecticut, and in 2009 Blue Sky Studios moved there from New York. This major computer animation film studio is best known for its *Ice Age* franchise.

Today, the state is focused on growing new, cutting-edge media opportunities. It offers incentives like tax credits for digital media companies that move to the state. This has led many animation and video game companies to set up in Connecticut. These high-tech businesses bring great jobs and additional money to the state.

The Connecticut State
Capitol opened in 1879.

5 Government

The people of Connecticut take a great deal of pride in their history of self-government. Since the Fundamental Orders of 1639, the government has answered to local voters. Today, the state is divided into "towns" that act as local governments. This system is similar to other states in New England, but quite different from the rest of the country. State lawmakers also meet in Hartford to made decisions that affect all local towns.

Local Government

Connecticut has 169 towns. Each likes to be as independent as possible. People participate in town meetings and decide how a town should spend its money and run its affairs. This is called home rule. Local control and the power of each person's vote are still important in Connecticut.

Voters in each Connecticut town elect people to represent them. These representatives sometimes go by different names, depending on the town's type of government. Some small towns call each of their representatives a "selectman." The representatives serve together on the board of selectmen. The board conducts

Danbury residents can share their views at city council meetings.

meetings throughout the year to discuss and vote on important issues that affect residents.

Larger towns and cities call their representatives "council members." They form a town or city council. Sometimes these towns also have a manager hired by the council to help run the town.

In some cities, voters elect a mayor. A mayor's power can vary. Depending on the city, the mayor can run the city or serve as a contact between the community and the local city board or council.

Connecticut has eight counties: Hartford, New Haven, Fairfield, Middlesex, Litchfield, Windham, Tolland, and New London. Counties are groups of towns and cities located near one another. Unlike most states, Connecticut does not have county governments. Towns and cities like their independence, so they often do not place great importance on working together to create and support legislation that goes beyond their local area.

The Branches of Government

Connecticut's state government is structured like the US government. It has three parts, or branches. The three branches coexist so that one branch does not have too much power.

The Executive Branch

Dannel Malloy became governor of Connecticut in 2011.

The executive branch includes the governor, lieutenant governor, secretary of state, and treasurer. The governor either approves or vetoes (rejects) laws passed by the legislature. Approved laws are enforced by the governor and other executive agencies. The governor also appoints state officials and manages the state budget, which determines where the state spends its money. Governors are elected for four-year terms.

Connecticut representatives at work in 2018

The Legislative Branch

The state house of representatives and the state senate form the Connecticut General Assembly, the state's legislative branch. **Legislators** propose and vote on laws for the state. There are 36 state senators and 151 state representatives. Senators represent larger areas than representatives, who focus more on smaller, local areas. All are elected for two-year terms.

The Judicial Branch

The judicial branch includes a system of courts that make legal decisions on many levels. They decide whether people accused of crimes have broken a law. They rule on disputes between individuals or companies. In addition, the courts can decide if state laws are legal under the Connecticut constitution. The judicial system includes superior courts that handle most criminal trials and lawsuits brought by one citizen against another. If someone loses a court decision, they can appeal (ask for the decision to be changed), first to appellate courts and then to the Supreme Court of Connecticut.

Raymond E. Baldwin Courthouse is part of the superior court system.

Creating Laws

State legislators propose laws (called bills until they are passed) to address state issues. Sometimes the ideas behind a bill come from the state's residents. A senator or representative must introduce the bill in his or her own house. Then, a committee in that house will discuss and perhaps alter the bill. If the committee approves the bill, it goes to all the members of the same house. If members vote to approve it, the bill moves to the other house.

Members in the second house then discuss the bill. If they also agree, it goes to the governor to be approved. If the second house decides to revise the bill and then approves it, the revised version may go back to the first house for another vote. In some cases, members from both houses get together to merge different versions of the same bill passed by each house. Then both houses must vote to approve the new common version.

When a bill passed by both houses gets to the governor, he or she can accept or reject it. When the governor accepts it, it becomes law. If the governor rejects it and vetoes the bill, it can still become a law if two-thirds of the members in each house vote to override the veto. Sometimes a bill can become law if the governor takes no action and neither accepts nor rejects it.

The aftermath of the tragic shooting in Sandy Hook demonstrates the way that laws are passed in the state. On December 14, 2012, twenty-six people—twenty students and six adults—were shot and killed at the Sandy Hook Elementary School in Newtown, Connecticut.

The Connecticut legislature reacted quickly. First, a task force of legislators set out to determine ways to prevent future mass school shootings. They decided that a change to Connecticut's gun laws would help. After long legislative sessions that sometimes lasted well into the night, the state's house of representatives and senate both passed bipartisan gun control legislation. Bipartisan means that the bill had the support of both the Democratic and the Republican Parties.

Following the votes, the senate and house merged their different bills into one final version, which was then signed by the

A memorial to the victims of the Sandy Hook shooting

Staying Informed

One responsibility of citizens is to stay informed about political issues. In a **democracy**, it is the people who hold power. They vote for people to represent them and run the government in a way that they agree with. But if the people do not know about the issues facing their community, they cannot do their job properly.

In the early days of the United States, citizens had to rely on in-person meetings and newspapers to learn about what was happening around them. They would go to local town hall meetings, chat with neighbors, and share newspapers and pamphlets.

Today, it is even easier to stay informed. Smartphones and computers allow people to access the news at the click of a button. However, this comes with at a cost. Websites and social media accounts can give inaccurate information. It is the responsibility of people reading them to distinguish fact from fiction.

Connecticut's official websites and official social media accounts help citizens learn about key issues the state faces.

One way to do this is to get information from official sources. Both the Democratic and Republican Parties of Connecticut have official Twitter accounts: @CTDems and @CTGOP. Posts that appear on them should be based in fact. Of course, both accounts try to post information that makes their party look good. This is why it can be useful to follow both parties. You can compare what they each say and try to see through the spin to the real issues in the middle.

state's governor, Dannel Malloy. The signing completed a three-month process that began shortly after the December 14 massacre.

Laws for Changing Times

New laws are passed all the time. They reflect changing attitudes and new realities. In 2014, Governor Malloy signed a law to increase the state's minimum wage. The minimum wage is the lowest amount that a worker can be paid. The law increased it from $8.70 an hour to $10.10 over the following three years. The last increase took place on January 1, 2017. This increase reflected the fact that living expenses in the state had risen over the years. The old minimum wage was no longer enough, so a new law needed to be passed.

Another change that took place in 2017 was an overhaul of "handicapped" parking signs. Previously, the image on the signs was of an upright figure in a wheelchair—like the ones found in most other states. But the signs were updated in 2017 to a new image of a figure leaning forward in the act of pushing the wheelchair. The new image portrayed people with disabilities as active and independent. This law reflected the evolving attitude toward people with disabilities across the state. It is an example of why laws need to be rewritten and updated. As society moves forward, new laws are required.

New reserved parking signs in Connecticut show people with disabilities as active and independent.

Glossary

abolitionist   A person who opposed slavery and worked to have it abolished, or ended.

agricultural   Relating to farming.

automated   Made with machines rather than through human labor.

democracy   A form of government in which people choose leaders by voting.

diverse   Having variety.

emancipation   The freeing of slaves.

epidemic   An outbreak of a disease that spreads quickly.

financial   Relating to money or banks.

foliage   The leaves of plants.

industrialization   The development and use of factories and machines.

legislator   Lawmaker; a member of the house or senate at the state or federal level.

maritime   Relating to the ocean or sea.

prosecuted   To be taken to court and accused of breaking a law.

prosperous   Successful or rich.

provisions   Supplies; military provisions include food, drink, ammunition, and weaponry.

recession   When the economy declines for a certain length of time.

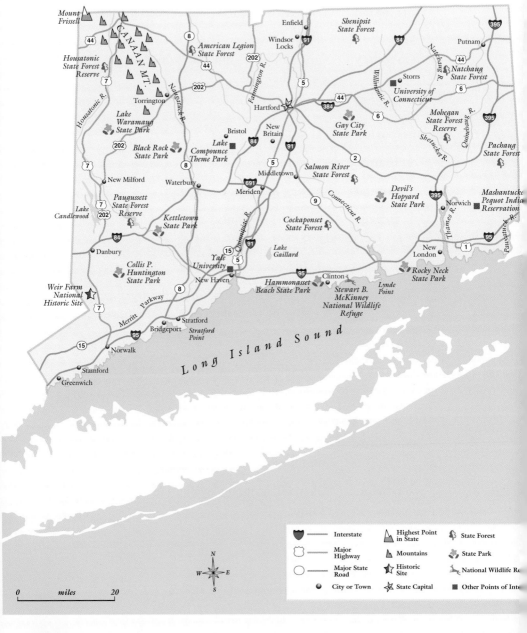

Mount Frissell

CANAAN MT.

44

Housatonic State Forest Reserve

7

8

American Legion State Forest

202

44

Enfield

Windsor Locks

91

Shenipsit State Forest

84

Putnam

44

Natchaug State Forest

6

Mohegan State Forest Reserve

395

Pachaug State Forest

Torrington

Lake Waramaug State Park

202

202

Black Rock State Park

8

Lake Compounce Theme Park

Bristol

New Britain

84

91

5

Hartford

44

384

Storrs

University of Connecticut

6

Gay City State Park

2

Naugatuck R.

Willimantic R.

Shetucket R.

Quinebaug R.

New Milford

7

Paugussett State Forest Reserve

202

Waterbury

Meriden

691

5

Middletown

Salmon River State Forest

Devil's Hopyard State Park

395

Norwich

Mashantucket Pequot India Reservation

Lake Candlewood

Kettletown State Park

9

Cockaponset State Forest

Connecticut R.

Thames R.

Danbury

84

Collis P. Huntington State Park

15

Yale University

5

91

Lake Gaillard

95

Clinton

New London

95

1

Weir Farm National Historic Site

7

8

New Haven

Hammonasset Beach State Park

Lynde Point

Rocky Neck State Park

Merritt Parkway

Stewart B. McKinney National Wildlife Refuge

Bridgeport

Stratford

Stratford Point

15

Norwalk

95

Stamford

Greenwich

Long Island Sound

N W E S

0 miles 20

	Interstate		Highest Point in State		State Forest
	Major Highway		Mountains		State Park
	Major State Road		Historic Site		National Wildlife R...
	City or Town		State Capital		Other Points of Inte...

76 • Connecticut

Map Skills

1. What body of water lies to the south of Connecticut?

2. What two roads meet in Norwalk?

3. What mountain is in the northwest corner of the state?

4. What town is between Hammonasset Beach State Park and Stewart B. McKinney National Wildlife Refuge?

5. What river runs through Torrington?

6. What town is the University of Connecticut located in?

7. What two towns are on the Thames River?

8. Which two interstates run through Hartford?

9. Which city is about 20 miles west of Clinton?

10. What is the southernmost town in Connecticut?

Answers

1. Long Island Sound
2. US Route 7 and Interstate 95
3. Mount Frissell
4. Clinton
5. Naugatuck River
6. Storrs
7. Norwich and New London
8. Interstate 84 and Interstate 91
9. New Haven
10. Greenwich

More Information

Books

Burgen, Michael. *Connecticut.* Danbury, CT: Scholastic Library
Publishing, 2018.

Garcia, Tracy J. *Eli Whitney.* New York: Rosen Publishing Group, Inc., 2013.

Otfinoski, Steve. *Exploring the Connecticut Colony.* North Mankato, MN:
Capstone Press, 2016.

Websites

Connecticut Government
https://portal.ct.gov/government
Connecticut's government website links to information
about elected officials and recent issues.

No Child Left Inside
https://www.ct.gov/ncli
The website for the state's No Child Left Inside program provides
information about events for children in Connecticut and information
about the program to inspire children to go outside more.

Visit CT
http://www.ctvisit.com
The official website for the Connecticut Office of Tourism
provides many ideas for fun activities in the state.

Index

Page numbers in **boldface** refer to images. Entries in **boldface** are glossary terms.